Ali McClure's
FingerTips

TALKING TOGETHER...

The tools to talk about learning,

The tools to learn through talking

By the Award Winning Author of
'Making it Better for Boys'

Ali McClure
e: office@alimcclure.co.uk
w: www.alimcclure.co.uk
t: 07816 408 181

@AliMcClureEP

Published in 2024 by Vantage Publishing Limited
9 Chestnut Suite, Guardian House, Godalming, Surrey GU7 2AE

www.vantagepublishing.co.uk

ISBN: 978-1-8383469-8-0

TALKING TOGETHER...

The tools to talk about learning,

The tools to learn through talking

FingerTips- The language of learning... for life

Finding the right words is not easy, at any age. If we are in a new situation, a difficult situation or we need more time.. As adults, we expect children to be able to tell us what they have done, what they have learned, but do we empower them with the tools to use and the words that work and ways to start simply, start today then 'embed it into their everyday'?

As the adults around them, are we confident in our own learning conversations? Are we confident with sharing these strategies with parents and professionals, carers and colleagues? These conversations help our children to speak out and shine, they promote oracy and agency

Do we make time for talking together- with our children, about our children, and among out children? Do we show that we care about what matters most to them, their learning and their feelings?

Do we then encourage them to dive deeper? Are they equipped for reflecting on the process and the progress; not just the what, but truly understanding how they have learned it-and how they can learn in the future- the metacognition?

Do we help them build their beginnings, have the questions to consolidate their connections and, as they grow and we grow with them, have the skills to take their learning further-next time and in the future?

Children of every age can struggle with the language skills, the right words or more importantly the right questions to ask themselves? How can we help them to grow this reflective vocabulary and always have it to hand? Whether we are working with children, reflecting on our own learning or working with adults - in any context in life we are always learning, we are all learners.

This book is written about a child and us, the adults around them, but we all are children at heart. Whatever age you are, whatever the age of the person you are nurturing or teaching, coaching or managing...

FingerTips empowers everyone to start simply – and that's just what you can do today.

Ali McClure's
FingerTips

TALKING TOGETHER...

The tools to talk about learning,

The tools to learn through talking

WHAT IS FINGERTIPS?

FingerTips is a 'talking together' tool for anyone learning at any age

FingerTips is five fingers, five questions... the tools to talk about learning with a depth of reflection

FingerTips is a simple tool that nurtures important learning skills and strategies for learning and for life - oracy, agency and meta-cognition, confidence, self-regulation and self-esteem

FingerTips is a flexible and unforgettable reflective learning tool for every learner, and those who teach, guide or mentor them.

FingerTips is an empowering approach for assessment and evaluation, for reflection and connection, for day to day dialogues and for difficult discussions

FingerTips is simple, supporting and sustainable. It is effective from before they can speak until they run their own businesses

FingerTips is an adaptable approach that anyone can use to talk about learning and to learn through talking - and listening of course. In learning and in life, in all ages of education and in any trade or profession, In education, family life or any trade or profession

FingerTips helps learners start simply, understand their learning and have the words that work to take their learning further than you would ever have thought possible.

WHY DO WE NEED FINGERTIPS?

Talking together is becoming an endangered practice. Everyone's lives are busy and screens suck us in, children and adults alike. Childhoods are crammed with so many things, the curriculum too, but conversations are few and far between. When busy families get precious time together they are too exhausted to truly connect- or they simply don't have the space or the strategies.

So many children are starting school with fewer words that ever before, and not just fewer words, social skills and self-regulation are also often a struggle.

FingerTips helps everyone by giving them the tools for

Talking together,

> Learning together

> > Growing together

- It starts simply so its easy to share
- It supports reflection and connection
- It supports oracy, agency and metacognition

Self-regulation and executive function are complex skills, but ones that help our children succeed in school, in social skills and in life. Some of the strands of these from the Education Endowment Fund's Evidence Store's recent guidance shows the crucial importance of these skills. They point to approaches which are so easily met by embedding **FingerTips** into our 'everyday' (These strategies may be suggested for Early Years but they are most certainly skills for learning from building the beginnings right through to the board of directors!)

Teaching self-monitoring and self-awareness	This approach involves the educator helping children to develop an awareness of their own thoughts and emotions , including how their feelings can influence their actions and vice- versa	<ul><li>Memory prompts</li><li>Teaching strategies</li><li>Naming and labelling</li><li>Making links between experiences and events</li><li>Suggesting</li></ul>
Creating a community of collaborative learners	This approach involves educators faciliatating children's collaborative learning as they work towards shared goals	<ul><li>Co-ordinating</li><li>Questioning</li><li>Providing a menu of strategies</li><li>Signposting</li><li>Being a co-player</li><li>Refocussing</li><li>Recapping</li></ul>
Promoting talk about learning	This approach involves educators encouraging talk that enables children to plan, monitor and reflect on their thinking and learning. This includes how they plan to approach or adapt an activity and evaluating it afterwards	<ul><li>Thinking aloud</li><li>Planning and sequencing</li><li>Evaluating</li><li>Making links</li><li>Recapping</li><li>Using mistakes to learn</li><li>Predicting</li><li>Drawing attention</li></ul>

WHAT DOES FINGERTIPS DO?

FingerTips builds connections. It helps learners make links that help them understand what they have learned and how they, as a unique individual, learns best. It helps other learners around them learn from their learning journey, and their effective reflections

FingerTips builds connections between people, helping us better understand what matters most to them. It helps us to dive into the depth of learning and how it makes them feel, and how we can help them most.

FingerTips is a flexible and unforgettable reflective learning tool for every learner. It empowers them to explain and share with 'those who need to know what it is they need to grow'. With a little practice it soon becomes an important and indispensable part of 'everybody's everyday'.

FingerTips equips and empowers everyone with the tools to use, the words that work and the skills for

Talking together,

Learning together

Growing together

What is FingerTips?
FingerTips is a reflective learner's talking tool.

Simply based on the five fingers of your hand, this supportive and sustainable tool empowers everyone, whatever their age, in 'talking toghether' reflecting on their learning, behaviour and learning behaviours and to have the language to share this learning with others, to bring this learning to life. It soon becomes an essential part of 'everybody's everyday'

It equips everyone with the words that work (oracy) and the tools to use to understand their learning (metacognition)

'The tools to talk about learning, The tools to learn through talking'

Know it, Grow it and Show it!
It gives them the confidence to own their own learning, behaviour and learning behaviours and to share this, helping others to grow too.

It makes being successful achievable and believable for every child. It equips every learner and those who lead them to be reflective and effective

The conversation cues, catalyst questions and discovery dialogues help them to believe in themselves. If we embrace and embed this seemingly simple approach into our 'everyday' it equips us to empower them to own their own learning and that 'You too can do it!'. It gives us all the language of learning for life.

CONTENTS

FingerTips

CONVERSATION CUES
The gestures made by each finger on your hand - they prompt the child to reflect on a specific aspect of their learning process.

DISCOVERY DIALOGUES
Dialogues between adult and child or child and child that use the conversation cues and catalyst questions to discover more about what was important to the child in the process and progress of their learning.

CATALYST QUESTIONS
Specific simple questions which open up opportunities for conversation to delve deeper - to whatever level is appropriate for that child and their current level of maturity, skill and confidence in reflection.

REFLECTIVE RESPONSES
The considered responses to catalyst questions about children, with children or among children- or the adults around them .

EMBEDDING INTO THE EVERYDAY
The way to make the **FingerTips** approach part of your everyday practice, using it flexibly to meet your needs.

REFLECTIVE LEARNING TOOL
What we call our hand when using the **FingerTips** approach. 'Let's use our Reflective Learning Tool'.

What sets **FingerTips** apart is its versatility, flexibility and accessibility. It is so simple to implement:

- You can choose to start simply so you could start today, sharing a catalyst question with a child, with a parent, with a colleague.
- You could choose to give the learner full agency, free choice in how they respond - 'What are you particularly proud of today?' or 'What made you smile inside?'
- Or you could narrow the focus, own the agenda by asking 'Thinking of your experiment today - what gives you pride inside?'
- When reflecting on a child's learning or the context we have created around them we could narrow the focus, 'Thinking of their sensory needs - what are they particularly proud of? What are we particularly proud of? '
- If you are wanting a deeper understanding, to know what are the roots of their learning, what is beneath their behaviours then skip ahead to the Diving Deeper section.

If you are wanting to get stuck in straight away – go straight ahead - with Starting Simply.

SECTION A

STARTING SIMPLY

CONVERSATION CUE NO. 1 - THUMBS UP

What are you particularly proud of?
Lots of people relate this gesture with 'good' or 'great.' Children tend to know that this thumbs up is a sign of something positive. Simply tweaking your language when you ask this question makes such a difference - the specific subtleties of the words are important.

When you are asking about their day, their picture, their lesson, instead of asking a child 'What are you good at?' ask them specifically *'What are you particularly proud of?'*

A child is likely to stop and think *'I am proud of the leaves'*;

This then gives you an opportunity to ask, *'What is it about the leaves that you are proud of?'*.

Depending on their maturity as a reflective learner, their answers are likely to be quite varied. It could be 'They are green' or 'They are pointy'.

Either way, the child has had to delve into their depths of vocabulary and draw on previous learning to find the word to describe the leaves.

If a child is non-verbal or their language (or confidence) is not sufficiently developed, you can reflect on the responses they might give if they were able to answer. We are often surprised at how much we can still discover about their learning.

A more practiced child or perhaps an older child might respond with:

'I like the detail in the leaves. It took me a long time to draw them.'

or:

'I spent time on the shading of the leaves. It shows how the light was falling on them.'

You may have noticed that whatever the child's response, it gives you an opportunity to delve deeper into their understanding of learning, helping them in the complex craft of appraising their process, not just the product

You might respond with 'What was it that took a long time to draw?' and before you know it, you have a **DISCOVERY DIALOGUE** taking place. All from one simple question; 'What were you particularly proud of?'

The questions in the **FingerTips** Talking Together… approach are simple but specific. They are **CATALYST QUESTIONS**; they lead on to further opportunities for discussing learning and learning behaviours based on what is important to that child.

You can narrow the focus by asking about their picture or their performance or with no specific context, you can simply ask 'What are you particularly proud of?' and be prepared for the answer to be quite different from what you were anticipating. What this does is gives the child agency, the opportunity to share what matters most to them. It also gives them and the adults around them the words that work to talk about it- the beginnings of oracy- talking about learning, learning through talking.

What these questions are not are checklist questions; the kind often used for summative or closed assessment or for checking whether our recipe for learning that day has been followed- they make more connections, they open up more opportunites…

Because the questions are based on what is important to that child, other children will know that the conversation is likely to be interesting, that they will hear things that relate to them, and they know they can learn from. Children tune in to these **DISCOVERY DIALOGUES** and **REFLECTIVE RESPONSES** much more than questions asked by adults, the ones they know that you already know the answers to. With the FingerTips approach you will genuinely discover things about how your children are thinking and learning; more importantly they are able to discover how they learn for themselves, and they will begin to use metacognition.

> 'Metacognition is **awareness and control of thinking for learning.**
> Strong metacognitive skills have the power to impact
> student learning and performance.'
> London School of Economics April 2021

Each of the **CONVERSATION CUES** (otherwise known as fingers) can be used as prompts,
with no concerns for misinterpretation. They can be used alone or in any combination.
They also each have extra depth which comes later in this book,
but for now, let us stick with simple.

Process and Progress

We have started with the thumbs up; *'What are you particularly proud of?'*

When we are modelling this to the children, sharing with them what *we* are particularly proud of, it is important that we sometimes focus on what we have tried, the process and the progress, not just the product. We feed back by saying 'I feel pride inside that I tried… making a paper plane that flies straight.'

Through these modelled examples, it helps the children to reflect on the feeling that it is also OK to be proud of trying something and then deciding it is not the right way for them. That trial and error on the journey of learning is something to be proud of in itself. With this approach, children begin to notice for themselves that the journey is rewarding, rather than expecting external recognition or relying on rewards.

Perhaps the thumbs up sign could be held in the centre of the chest to reinforce this: that we feel that pride; that happy emotion inside.

This approach can also help younger children who find the concept of feeling 'proud' a little abstract. *'I feel pride inside'* is only one small step on from *'I feel a smile inside.'*

'I feel a smile inside that I tried... touching the lizard.'
(Even if a child is not able to say it for themselves, we can observe
'What makes them smile inside?')

The connections you are helping the children to build are between the physical gesture they make with their hand **CONVERSATION CUES** and their **REFLECTIVE RESPONSE** – their reflection on what and how they learn. It is important to model the gesture each time you ask a **CATALYST QUESTION** and to encourage the child to use it when they are responding. This pays dividends when the practice becomes embedded as you will begin to see children using the gestures in their everyday interactions. Whether they are talking to a partner, feeding back to a larger group or the whole class, they simply use their FingerTips to make talking about their learning, and learning through talking make sense.

But the incredible thing about this tool is its flexibility, its adaptability, and its longevity. It only needs one finger at a time, and it does not matter which one you begin with. Choose whichever one works best for you, for your children and for the situation you are in. Use it with the phrase 'Particularly Proud' or use it without, to make it work for children who use their home language and those who use none.

Try it out in your daily discussions with children but please let it come naturally. It should never be a drill or a drudge. When it is allowed to evolve it becomes embedded in your practice, into your 'everyday' and a tool to turn to. It equips and empowers.

When you and the adults around them are practiced in 'Particularly Proud, and ready to explore more', later sections will empower you to take this topic to greater depths.

CONVERSATION CUE NO. 2 – THE POINTING FINGER

The Pointing Finger
This finger is the index finger, and the child points it politely at the person or the thing that helped in their learning today. So, the **CATALYST QUESTION** is *'Who helped you today?'* or *'What helped you today?'*

Who helped you today?
A child may simply respond *'You did!'* That is always reassuring to know, but it also could be what they thought you were hoping to hear! So dive deeper: *'How did I help you?'*

> *You helped me by getting me to touch the leaf.'*

> *'How did that help you?'*

> *'When I could feel that the leaf was spiky, then I knew how to draw the pointy bits.'*

Of course, an older child or even an adult would have a more mature response, but you can see how this simple starting point can develop with the child and grow their language for learning and reflective learning skills along the way.

What helped you today?
'What helped you today?' is the other question this pointing finger prompts.

A child might answer:

> *'Having a magnifying glass helped me to see what the leaf really looked like'*

> or

> *'Looking at pictures of how other people have drawn different shaped leaves.'*

The power of this pointing finger prompt is that children come to expect that it is OK to have something or someone to help them, but not to rely on all the time. Also, to begin to recognise the tools and tips which support their particular learning. As adults we are always up for a 'Top Tip', especially one that has worked well for someone we respect. Similarly, children are more likely to tune in to children like themselves sharing about who or what helped them in their learning.

This approach also builds a culture of offering and seeking support, not only building cognitive skills, but building social and communication skills too!

Enabling and Empowering Adults
So far, we have looked at the benefits for the children. However, when I am working with teachers at the start of their career, they often are looking for ways to find out how best to support children whose learning is slower to grow. Building regular **DISCOVERY DIALOGUES**

means that children begin to reveal specifically what helps them to learn. As the enabling adults, you can be empowered to know what to provide for that child, whether it is a specific interaction or intervention, or that it prompts you to provide provocations and appropriate props that are perfectly matched to the needs of that child, right now.

This *'What helped you?'* and *'Who helped you?'* is just as much about extending learning as enabling learning. It is a regular reminder that deploying just the right resources can be the very thing that child needs to take their learning further, growing skills, strategies and confidence for themselves.

CONVERSATION CUE NO. 3 – THE MIDDLE FINGER

The third finger is obviously the middle finger - but don't worry, it is polite! The gesture is that of a bumpy road, so hold out your hand flat with the palm facing downwards and curl all the fingers, except the middle one into your palm. Now hold that shape with the longest finger pointing away from you. This finger represents the longest journey.

The longest journey

The journey of learning is always the longest journey. However much you have learned or however old you get, it is never complete. There will always be bumps along the way. Our job as educators is to empower and equip children to bounce back from those bumps and to know that this resilience is an essential part of learning. The upper surface of our middle finger represents this beautifully. It is uneven, it is bumpy and there is a knuckle in the middle. A place to pause and appraise the progress made, the problems overcome, and the skills learned to help us next time.

So how do we use this with the children?

Avoiding 'wrong'

Please avoid the word 'wrong'. Wrong is finite and curtails creative solutions. Also, wrong is based on the opinion of others, and we do not want to promote children relying on our approval. Neither do we want the children to feel judged, rather to recognise and respond to the challenges for themselves. Everyone makes mistakes and encounters problems, but it is how we deal with them that makes the difference.

I just love how, when children are sharing their reflections using this finger, they smile as they are sharing their problems, because they know they are going to get to share how they solved it.

Tricky and Tackling it

> *'I found this tricky, but I tried that and now I know how to start next time.'*

> *'I had a problem with this, and I tried that. It helped a bit but not enough. I knew I needed to ask Mrs. Jenson for some support.'*

It is so powerful as it helps them to know what they need to help them succeed. What a skill this is for any of us. At any point in our lives.

Danger Zone!

The skill of the person curating the question is in never simply asking 'What did you find tricky?' and stopping there. This leaves the child vulnerable and exposed, feeling bad about themselves.

Always, *always* use the longer **CATALYST QUESTION**: the one that enables a resolution. Never leave them with the thought of what they found tricky - with no resolution.

> *'What did you find tricky and how did you tackle it?'*

> or

> *'What problem did have today and how did you make progress to overcome it?'*

> or

> *'What did you struggle with and how did you solve it?'*

(It also is empowering to ask, *'How did that make you feel?'* taking the opportunity to promote the language of emotion and helping the children connect their feelings)

Question and Resolution

The question must always lead the learner towards the resolution. Have the children feel the bumps on the back of their finger as they describe it.

> *'What did you find tricky and how did you tackle it?'*

'The trickiest part was getting the shading right, the marks were always too strong, too dark.'

> *'How did you tackle it ?'*
> (And you can be confident they have, or they wouldn't be sharing it with you)

> *'I used a softer pencil. My grandad showed me that pencils are soft as well as hard –*
> *he draws pictures of birds and always uses a special pencil –*
> *and he's the best at drawing birds, especially robins!'*

It is at this point that children often tell us more about their experiences, that they use strategies that they have learnt at home, in different situations or that they have learnt from others around them.

The whole FingerTips discovery dialogue enables the child not only to have the words that work - oracy, but the opportunity to talk about 'what matters most to them', the agency to own their conversation , their responses and, gradually, but eventually- their learning .

Depth of reflection

Oh, my goodness! As the adult, what have you learned about the child's important relationships, your resourcing in your class or setting and maybe even about drawing technique! This is so much more than was in anyone's intent or learning objective. This depth of reflection will really make a difference to enabling and extending the learning of this child and of so many others in the future.

We share the same struggles

Perhaps more importantly, is how interesting the **REFLECTIVE RESPONSE** is to the other children who are keen to learn to improve their drawing skills. They are learning from a child expert and it is so much more powerful to learn from positive peers in a way that makes them feel that they, too can do it. It is also good to discover that many people who seem to find things easy also have struggles and need to find solutions. We have the same struggles that they do so we must be OK!

CONVERSATION CUE NO. 4 - THE RING FINGER

Repetition of the Right Thing
The fourth finger is the ring finger. A ring is a circle, a shape that rotates, rolls, repeats. The conversation cue that it prompts is concerned with repetition. Not just repetition for repetition's sake, but repetition of the right thing. This 'right thing' is something that that child is ready and ripe to develop, that will help them be even more successful next time. The repetition is about routines, rhythms and rituals that are in their lives.

The reflection with this finger is probably a little more challenging for young children and will need some modelling before they are able to use it for themselves depending on the context there are two options for the catalyst question. One option is :

What have you repeated regularly that helped you...?
This question is great when you are reflecting on practice with the adults around the children. When talking to the children themselves I would go with-

What did you practise...?
The **CATALYST QUESTION** is *'What did you practise that helped you with your picture today?'*

> *'I took a sketch pad with me to the park with Grandad and practised drawing leaves of all different shapes'.*

> *'I practised drawing leaves really big with chalk on the big blackboard – it was easier to draw it when it was bigger'.*

Their **REFLECTIVE RESPONSE** might be as simple as *'I practised drawing'.* This is perfectly fine, the fact that this child has processed the question and offered an answer. Not only that, but if it promotes using just a little of their leisure time to practise the simple skill of drawing in amongst all the tempting distractions of our modern world, that has to be a good thing.

Successful people practise
Hearing from others, this **CONVERSATION CUE** also helps children to recognise that people who are successful have practised and continue to do so; they repeat the things which are right for them. This makes being successful all the more achievable and believable for every child, especially if they have previously felt judged or their self-belief has not been so strong.

Applying their practice
My favourite recollection of using this **CONVERSATION CUE** was with a group of six-to-seven-year-olds in a school where FingerTips was embedded.

At the end of a carefully-curated school sports day (a veritable minefield!), children were given the opportunity to reflect using the FingerTips tool. We started with the thumb and worked our way through the **CONVERSATION CUES** as the children were now very comfortable with this.

There were so many examples to share of feeling pride inside, knowing who and what helped them and how they solved their own struggles; a warm and wonderful feeling was flowing among the children.

I was loving it; seeing how the **FingerTips** reflective tool was having such a positive impact that I had not noticed that we were needing to get the children back for lunch. I decided to skip the ring finger and move on to the final finger. Then I noticed, one little girl was putting up her hand, desperately trying to get my attention.

So, I paused and asked Chloe what it was she wanted to share. She adamantly pointed out that I had missed out the ring finger - the repetition of the right thing - and that she had been practising. She was an able athlete, and, of her own volition, she had been practising the starts of races every day in the playground. She described the technique she used and how, today in the races, she had applied this practice; she was able to describe how this helped her do even better than she had done before. Everyone - all the children and adults were engrossed in her explanation and her pride in how her practice had made such a difference.

'You too can do it!'

This was infant P.E. Teaching the technique for starts of races had not come from me; this little girl's reflection was extending the learning of others and showing them an incredible and humble role model to help them strive for success in the future, to show them that 'You too can do it!'

CONVERSATION CUE NO. 5 - LINKED LITTLE FINGERS

Linked Learning
So on to the final finger - the little finger. Take your two little fingers, (put everything down first!) and link them together. The linking of the little fingers is the **CONVERSATION CUE** for linked learning.

The **CATALYST QUESTION** is:

'Choose one thing from your learning today that you will remember when you try this again.'

or

'What will you take away from today that you can use tomorrow?'

Some children call this their 'Pinky Promise' or simply their 'Linked Learning.' Although the phrase they use helps, it is less about what they call it and more about the prompt and positivity that this gesture generates.

'I will remember to use a magnifying glass in order to see the detail in what I am drawing'

'I will try using a 2B pencil to get softer shading'

and already you will find your children are making cognitive connections between what they will do and how it will help them.

Cognitive load - What chimes with them most?
If you and your children are practised in the FingerTips approach and are using all five fingers to reflect, there may well be too much to remember. We need to be mindful of cognitive load and, by allowing each child to choose the one thing that chimes with them most they are more likely to remember this and apply it.

Helping them make a start
When they next come to drawing, to running, to working in a group they can link their fingers and they can remember the one thing that will help them make a start- and that is exactly what they do... At the start of the next lesson or when approaching an activity, without a word, I link my little fingers and the children do the same. I will see pairs of children start to talk through what they learned the last time. Often, I don't even need to link my fingers to prompt - one child will do this, and the others will follow their lead - it has become automatic.

Knowing what they need to help them succeed
Having just one thing to remember, that they know will help them be successful, helps every child have the confidence to be a self-starter, to know where to begin - and sharing this language of learning, either with a partner or simply in their own head is such a positive start. They begin their learning knowing what they need to help them succeed. What more could you want!

EMBEDDING AND MOVING ON

Before you move on with FingerTIps, I recommend that you practise the simple strategies with your children, with your team or for yourself; helpful habits become embedded with practice.

Simple, supportive and sustainable
The strength in this strategy is that it is simple to implement, supportive and sustainable. There is no need to use all five of the FingerTips, introduce it using just one **CONVERSATION CUE**, one finger or your thumb and choose the one that feels right for you and those you have the privilege to know and grow.

The language of learning for life!
Only move on when you are ready. It is difficult to misinterpret so it is great to share with parents, older siblings, new team members - everyone can benefit from FingerTips – an easy to implement, shared and sustainable approach - empowering everybody to talk about learning and learn through talking, the very definition of oracy, the language of learning - for life!

SECTION B

DIVING DEEPER

BENEATH THE SURFACE OF LEARNING - Remember the Roots

Upskill our questioning
The real strength of the FingerTips strategy is that it works on many levels, it dives deeper. It helps us all to reflect and connect... with the roots of our learning, with our strengths and successes, with our process and progress, on our own or with each other! It helps us, the children and all who work with them to gain important insights into how they learn best and about their own understanding of their own learning. The simple strategy we have practised does this perfectly, however this is just the beginning. If we know the depth of what lies beneath the surface, this can equip and empower us to upskill our questioning, perhaps sometimes to steer the questioning into a targeted context.

Know it, grow it show it!
Whether it is learning, behaviour or learning behaviours we are considering, knowing what lies beneath really empowers us to know the whole child - to use that insight to fuel our interactions and interventions. Knowing what lies beneath the behaviour. We are then able to help each and every child to begin to see this for themselves have agency and begin to understand how they learn and to know it... to grow it ... to show it!

An underlying understanding
We know every child is individual and unique, and we see this above the surface but what we need in order to help them grow, is an underlying understanding, we need to use our FingerTips **CATALYST QUESTIONS** to help them to connect with the roots of their learning, begin to see what is beneath the surface...

Behaviour is simply how they show -
What it is they need to grow!

Simple but subtle
Just like a plant growing, this depth of understanding does not come overnight, it takes time and energy, getting to know each child as an individual.

These roots of learning are simple but subtle, they have been formulated based on a range of sound research and many of you will see links with Maslow's hierarchy, Stuart Shanker's 5 Domains of Self-Regulation and the categories used to analyse and assess Special Educational Needs.

They have been trialed in many contexts, from schools and nurseries, to tutoring and coaching from hairdressers to bricklayers.

So, whether the learners you are nurturing are colleagues in your workplace or children in your care, we will visit each root in turn to see how we can better understand how they can become more rooted in their learning, behaviour and learning behaviours. We will dig deep to discover how we learn and how we can empower them, whether they are building their beginnings, consolidate their connections or are ready to take their learning further.

ROOTS OF LEARNING – PHYSICAL AND SENSORY

Understanding exactly what they need
Even before a child can speak, watching how a child moves and using our **FingerTips** - Let's talk… reflective tool can really help us to understand exactly what they need to practice and what are their next steps.

Cranial-Caudal, Proximal-Distal
A child's physical development follows the pattern; Cranial to Caudal (head to tail) then Proximal to Distal (near to far). As tiny babies they start with being able to support the weight of their own head progressing onto core and upper body strength. When these are in place then the shoulder and hip pivots and connections can develop.

Only when these connections are established, and consolidated will the elbow pivots, the wrist pivots the palms and finally the fingers - the fine motor skills fall into place. It is simply common sense, after all the twigs on a tree cannot grow leaves until the trunk and limbs are sufficiently mature.

from Making it Better for Boys Ali McClure 2008

Is it surprising that they struggle?
The stages of physical development are something we specifically need to observe for, and help children to develop at the stage they are currently at. If coordinating from their shoulder is a challenge and we ask them to make marks using small movements, is it surprising that they struggle, or even shy away from the experience?

Shifting the focus from the fine motor
Our focus is often heavily on fine motor skills, but we must always remember the progression and the larger movements which come first. Other fine motor skills which can often be overlooked act as clues to the child's development needs: the eyes being able to track across a page, the muscles in the mouth being able to form sounds effectively, even the motor skills involved in toileting are physical roots which can impact on a child's learning and behaviour.

Don't leave out the lower limbs
We must not forget the lower limbs - the hip pivot, the knee pivot and the ankle pivot as, strangely enough, scooting, bouncing and balancing are key factors in children being ready to read and write, in being ready to learn.

Crossing the mid-line
The body is inextricably linked to the brain and, doing activities which cross the midline of the body helps build links between the two hemispheres of the brain.

Asking advice of the experts
There are all kind of other complexities to physical development and, if you have particular concern about a child, do ask the advice of a physiotherapist or an occupational therapist.

Exercise before expectation
Even as adults, taking some exercise if we are struggling to make a start on a tricky task can make a difference - exercise before expectation is a mantra that still serves me well; for myself and when I am working with children.

Often overlooked
Two other, often-overlooked aspects of physical development are important to be aware of:

Proprioception: Close your eyes, point your index finger and touch your nose. I am guessing you managed this without a mirror. This is proprioception, - your brain knowing where parts of your body are, without needing to look. This development usually comes as a child becomes more mobile, but some older children still struggle, and many children go through challenges with this as their body grows and their brain takes a while to re-learn where their limbs are.

Vestibular: This is named after the part of your inner ear concerned with balance. It is also linked with children who need to rock or spin- have you ever wondered why children love swings and roundabouts at the park? Older children who rock or spin may often also have particular or additional needs.

Struggling for space
Children with challenges in either of the above needs will struggle if they do not have enough space. They may bump into things or into others, they may be seen as 'clumsy' or 'careless' but if we look beneath the surface, we can often pinpoint a particular area where we can support. If we can use our FingerTips tool to gain an underlying understanding, then that depth can make a real difference.

Sensory sensations
Movement gives us sensory sensations and our senses are an aspect of the physical root which we need to consider.

Perceiving and receiving
We all perceive and receive the world in different ways and some of our senses are more heightened (hyper) or subdued (hypo) than others. If we can observe these subtleties in our

children, then we are in a better position to support them if they struggle. There are small adaptations we can make such as ensuring a child can see what we are showing them straight on (peripheral vision can sometime be a problem) or noticing that they struggle with bright lights. We can be alert to smells which may be a problem for them - one toddler hated the smell of the wood burner at his child-minder's, another loved the smell of a diffuser.

Sensitive senses?
We have all come across children who are sensitive to sounds - a little boy with poor tooth hygiene couldn't tolerate the sound of his electric toothbrush. The solution might be as simple as providing ear defenders in busy environments. Some children are less sensitive to sounds.

Children who don't do as they are asked straight away may have glue ear. They may have difficulties with filtering out background noise or hearing our voices clearly. They need us to be alert to these potential challenges and to make adaptations.

Children who are picky with their food might have particularly sensitive taste buds and children who seek out skin sensations - or shy away from them need us to be careful what we ask them to wear or to know that a shoulder rub can soothe them.

Sensory detectives
All children need to learn about their senses and explore in multi-sensory ways, but we must also need to be aware of what might be underpinning their behaviours or holding back their learning. Stuart Shanker says we need to become 'sensory detectives.'

Our roots of learning guide us in this, and with the **FingerTips** approach embedded this should become part of our daily diet.

Repeated needs
There are, however, children who show repeated sensory needs, then it is wise to seek some advice or specialist support, learning how best to help meet their needs and gradually help them learn how to support these for themselves.

Complex and comprehensive
Who would have thought that our physical needs were so complex and comprehensive - but actually, it is not that surprising, there are many aspects to an engine, and human beings are so much more complex than those.

Back to basics
But we have been busy with the details and forgotten about the basics - the everyday things which keep our engines running smoothly. Air, food, (with plenty of protein) and water are all things we need constant access to. Shelter, and clothing protect us, from danger and from the elements and don't forget... something all children need plenty of... sleep!

The human connection
The final physical need we will consider is touch, however, this kind of touch is a special brand. It is not just touch, it is Appropriate, Physical Touch (A,P,T,). It is a hand on the shoulder as you walk past. It is a back rub when they wake up, it is skin to skin with a young baby. It is as simple as a hug.

Babies orphaned in war time had all their basic physical needs met - food, shelter, warmth, sleep etc. Other orphaned children were cared for in a poor community. Their basic needs were simply met but the difference was, these babies were carried, cuddled and rocked, smiled at, sung to and soothed. It does not take an expert to work out which ones thrived. Human physical contact connects directly with our emotional needs too - and these are both key ingredients for each one of us be ready to grow.

ROOTS OF LEARNING - EMOTIONAL EQUILIBRIUM

Spotting the signs
How do we get to understand a child's emotional needs? Sometimes they are obvious - if they are angry or frustrated then others around them are often the first to know. If they are happy, this is lovely to see, but being excited can actually make them feel anxious. If they are sad, we would hope that we would notice, likewise if they were scared. There are so many emotions and so many complex ones.

Emotional Equilibrium
Emotions are complex – they rarely stay the same and are at the mercy of so many external influences. One thing we can do is help our children recognise their emotions, find the vocabulary to be able to vocalise their emotions and- begin to be able to come back to balance, to emotional equilibrium

Overwhelming emotions
Emotions can often become overwhelming, especially if we are trying to suppress them, rather than having the words to express them. FingerTips helps children connect their learning, their behaviours and their deep-seated feelings. It equips them with the words that work to express their emotions.

> *'I felt frustrated when I couldn't finish my construction, but then Jas helped me by finding the right-sized blocks'*

'The context of the child'
Helping children recognise their emotions, big or small, and having words to express them as they grow is empowering; but seeing the bigger picture, knowing the impact of the environment around a child, the energy around them is so important . It is about reflecting on our role in this- sometimes not the most comfortable thing to do; but It is about really getting to know that child and what matters most to them - their background, their family - what a wise educational leader in Mexico Ivan Galindo calls 'The context of the child.'

Take time and make time
Our context and the challenges around us as adults, make a real difference to how present we can be when connecting with a child. When we say they are 'attention seeking', very often it is simply 'connection seeking'. If a child knows we are available, if we are predictably patient, and present- if they know that we listen, with our eyes and our ears, with our bodies, and amongst the busyness, if we take time and make time. This helps them to know and to see that they can trust us and feel safe to share. Very few people will find the words to open up and speak of their emotions effectively when they are in the middle of them. They are unlikely to communicate effecively 'in a corridor' literally or figuratively. Calm time spent together is much more likely to give us an insight into how they feel and an opportunity to appropriately explore what might be behind these feelings. It can also help them to find ways to return to calm, to their emotional equilibrium.

Reflect, Protect, Connect

I learned many lessons in raising my children, and still do. One of these was the connection of the car journey. Having one to one, uninterrupted time, alongside them with no particular pressure to talk (this detail is important - it is not an opportunity to interrogate!). Unpressured time in parallel often leads to conversations which give us glimpses of what matters most to them, of their emotions, their deep-seated feelings and what might be the causes. Dog walks, engineering projects, crafting, cooking and playing alongside all enable us to have these encounters. These connections are more likely to happen at times when the adults have fewer children, fewer challenges and are able to focus.One to one time is particularly powerful. These connections and conversations are much more likely to happen when the adults are calm, when the energy they are emitting, either consiously or unconsciously is warm and welcoming, is comforting and calm.

Do our environments lend themselves to these connections - cosy spaces and happy faces, places where they feel warm and welcome, where they feel sufficiently protected to be able to connect? A simple prompt that helps me work towards these emotional connections is:

Reflect,
Protect,
Connect.

My favourite opportunities for really getting to know a child, or an adult for that matter are often connected with food - not sugary treats but either preparing food together, alongside each other with a purpose and something nice to share when we are done, or simply sitting and eating with a child. Its less about the food, more about the oppportunities it opens up

I did this recently with a group of six-year-olds. It was so lovely, getting to find out what they were looking forward to as they transition to their new schools, finding out how they were feeling- not twenty questions but a calm, friendly, two-way conversation. Even in five minutes I was able to discover so much about what is important to them - and them to know just a little more about me - a human connection.

Emotional roots embedded

Looking back at our entire **FingerTips** talking together tool, we might think we are helping children to reflect on their learning, but much of its power is through helping children to also reflect on and connect with their emotions. Helping children find the words, and to focus on how they feel, alongside finding ways of returning to their emotional equilibrium are embedded throughout the **FingerTips** approach. We can begin to embed these **FingerTips** phrases into our everyday interactions, modelling powerful patterns of language even before children are ready to engage with the language of this simple talking together tool. This way they begin to reflect on their emotions without even noticing - and gradually grow the language of learning to describe their emotions for themselves.

'I feel pride inside…'

'I am particularly proud of' or 'I feel pride inside' helps children to reflect on what makes them feel good, what makes them smile - in fact when introducing this conversation cue, I am sure to smile while making the gesture and sometimes use the phrase 'I feel a smile inside…' or 'It makes me shine inside that I tried…'

It also gives children the chance to hear from and reflect on the emotions of others, and how they can interact with them. Learning is often more powerful when it comes from their peers and, when reflecting effectively is embedded into what we ordinarily do, this supports the learning of all children, especially those with additional needs.

Happiness and warmth

'Who helped me?' or *'What helped me?'* enables children to reflect on that feeling of happiness and warmth when someone cares; when a friend holds out a hand when they need it most. It helps them feel a sense of success when they have solved their own problem, finding the right tool for the task.

It helps them gradually develop empathy, knowing how being helped and supported makes them feel makes it more likely that they will reach out to help and support others.

'Today I helped Kira by letting them use my special pencil.'

Starting too soon?

You are the expert, the educator, and if you don't think your children are yet ready for the **FingerTips** approach, then start gradually and gently. One simple catalyst question is all it takes and each one is so simple to share. It's also a lovely way to start within families as every member can contribute and reap the benefits from being part of the conversation and becoming companions in their learning:

Talking Together...
Learning Together...
Growing Together...

Counting kindnesses

'Counting kindnesses' can be as simple as a conversation at circle time, mealtime or after an outdoor session. It helps children to become tuned in to these feelings of happiness, fulfilment and warmth and the actions which trigger these. Children simply talk about who was kind to them and how; then how they were kind to someone else. Keep it simple and short to start with.

As they become practised in counting kindnesses you could begin to model, encourage and maybe extend by adding in how that made you feel. *'Morgan was kind to me as she taught me the goodbye song. (It made me smile inside and made me feel happy).'*

It is also important to share how you were kind to someone else. *'I let Joe go through the door before me when he was carrying some books. (I felt happy that I had been able to see that this would help them)'.* You and your team know what they are ready for - so decide how long to spend, how deep to dive and when you are ready - share these phrases as a gentle start with parents - if the strategy reaches 'beyond the school gate' it has so much more impact.

Problems and Progress
The third and middle finger enables us to talk about what problems we had and what progress we made (remember that both must go together!) We begin to encourage children to know that it is OK to find things tricky, to feel discouraged, downhearted, a little sad, a little stuck. And the reason that this is OK is because we are helping them to be resilient and resourceful. *'I found it tricky to draw my face. It made me feel sad. Then I saw that Jenna was using a mirror. I tried it and I was able to do so much better and began to feel better. I still find it tricky, but I did OK'.* A young child is much more likely to say, *'I found it hard to draw my face - I got a mirror and it helped'.* It will take a time to get into the habit of reflecting on emotions and not everyone will feel comfortable to share. These (alongside those who overshare!) will be the ones on your radar, to spend some quiet time with, sliding in beside them where they are comfortable and starting with talking about what they are happy to talk about - or simply watching and listening until the time is right.

Observe, Wait, Listen
We need to make sure our interactions are meaningful; we need to use wise words and the Hanen team from Canada have a simple acronym to help us with this

The initial letters spell **OWL**, and like an owl; before we swoop, we need to take time, we need to watch and wait - it is amazing what we can learn without words!

Before children are ready for the 'longest journey' represented by the bumpy back of our middle finger the strategy of 'dealing with difficulties' might be a good starting point.

Dealing with Difficulties
When children are familiar with the 'counting kindnesses' approach, you will know when they are ready to begin to introduce 'dealing with difficulties.'

It happens in the same way, at a circle time, after a break or outdoor time, or over a meal or snack.

It is always important to start with the kindnesses, then gently add in the question *'What did you find difficult outdoors today?'*

Sharing will often rear its head as will friendships so be sure to deal with this sensitively.

'I wanted to play with the scooter, but Zainab had it!'

'I wonder how that made you feel?'

'It made me feel really, really cross'

'I could see that you felt that way- how did you deal with the difficulty?'

'I went to play with the construction until Zainab had finished'

You will find there is much modelling needed for this approach but be patient and persistent - only those with strong emotional role models at home or more mature emotional language will be ready to answer. Those who are not sharing are soaking it up - including children for whom English is an additional language, or those who are still building the beginnings of language for themselves.

If introduced consistently, you will be amazed how quickly this approach becomes part of the culture in your classroom or learning community. It also empowers the adults, and so many of us have previously not been practised in this open, honest and respectful way of communicating.

Behaviour is Communication - finding the words for their feelings
So often when children are feeling angry emotions, they do not have the language to express this, so they show it in their faces, and sometimes their fists!

Emotions are behind our actions
Emotions are behind so many of our actions - empowering children from an early age to find the right words for their feelings gives them a voice and this in itself is liberating for them. Children able to communicate with words rather than actions makes for a much calmer, more cooperative environment.

When they are feeling angry, unsettled or anxious it is scary for them - there are things going on inside them that they feel they have little control over - rather like we have no control over the the weather. Do young children have the words for what they feel inside?

Storm inside, struggle inside, steam inside

I feel:

a smile inside

sad inside

a storm/struggle inside

steam inside

© ALI MCCLURE EDUCATION AND PARENTING
WWW.ALIMCCLURE.CO.UK | @ALIMCCLUREP

FIVE

I feel a storm inside, I feel a struggle inside, I feel steam inside - these images are helpful to some children and others don't need them. You make that decision, however thinking of these images can help us reflect on how children are feeling if they are not able to use words. How many children have you seen that have a storm going on inside - we need to make things safe and give them strategies or simply wait for the storm to subside. If a child feels steam inside - then we can almost see this coming to a head - and we know that there needs to be a release before things will cool down again.

Repetition of the Right Thing - A Feeling of Fulfilment
A feeling of fulfilment, a feeling of ' I did that', a feeling of owning their own achievement are things that help children, not only to feel good about themselves and their own learning but also to have the energy and internal reserves to go on learning. Being able to see for themselves the impact of their practice on their progress gives them this. The fourth finger - the ring finger represents something we repeat that is going to make a difference - repetition of the right thing.

When children are ready to understand the impact of practice then, they will be able to feed back to others, to share with them *'I practised darting to catch a ball when it bounces and now, I am much better at playing throwing and catching with Maisie; it feels good to know that all that practice makes a difference'*

Of course, it starts simply - *'I practised catching'* but your catalyst questions are what make a difference to their depth, Using your insight and the context of the child helps you to know- what to ask, when to ask and how many questions are just enough. Having this feeling of fulfilment makes the child more confident and has a positive impact on their intrinsic motivation and their emotions.

Linked Learning - Feeling Confident to Make a Start –
(and to know why that strategy works for them)
Making a start is something many children struggle with, especially if they feel less confident, have with additional needs or challenges with their cognitive load. This can make them feel anxious. If they are lacking confidence or struggling to retrieve their previous learning, they may be slow to start, to make a decision as to what to do first. Being able to make a start is part of that complex skills of self-regulation

By using their linked little fingers to remember just one thing from their learning yesterday, they are giving themselves a simple prompt to help get them get started today. It might be as simple as recording their words on a sound button before they write them or knowing that putting the bigger blocks at the bottom will help their tower be more stable. They will have learned a strategy they can apply in many other situations. Feeling confident, not only to make a start but to begin to understand what helps them learn best (metacognition) equips and empowers them in knowing what they need to help them succeed.

How effective is the approach? The average impact of metacognition and self-regulation strategies is an additional seven months progress over the course of a year

Metacognition and self-regulation strategies can be effective when taught in collaborative groups so that learners can support each other and make their thinking explicit through discussion.

HOBBS AND BERNARD EDUCATION ENDOWMENT FOUNDATION OCT 21

Learning Tone – Energy and Environment
The last thing to share about the Emotional Equilibrium root of learning accents the important role of the adults - it is us who make the emotional environment for our children to grow and learn in.

Walking into a learning environment, it is perfectly possible to feel the energy, the learning tone, the relationships, the way that people interact with each other .

Even Before it Begins (EBB)
E: Our **ENVIRONMENT, ENERGY** and **EYE CONTACT** set the tone.
B: **BODY LANGUAGE** - so many messages before we even open our mouths
B: **BONDING** - The opportunities through the day to get to know each child and their context, - especially those who seem harder to reach - and to let them discover just a little about their adults.

FingerTips is about...

The **FingerTips** reflective learning tool is about reflecting and connecting in so many ways and, until we have the words that work for us, learning from the language of others.

It is about talking together, learning together, growing together

It is about self-esteem and recognising success for themselves

It is about resilience and resourcefulness.

It is about cooperation not comparison

It is about practice and perseverance.

It is about meetings and mentoring

It is about observation, conversation and coaching

It is about talking about learning, it is about learning through talking

It is about reflection and connection - for them, for others and for us.

It is about the language of learning... for life.

ROOTS OF LEARNING - SOCIAL SKILLS,
Self-Esteem and SELF-Regulation

Making collaborative connections - comfortable and confident
Our children need to feel comfortable with themselves before they will reach out to others. They need to feel good about themselves first- have strong self-esteem and the environment we establish can help them feel comfortable and confident in order to make connections. We can engineer opportunities that help them see their successes, help them tackle what is tricky- help them feel pride inside. It is good to reflect- what makes that child shine- inside and out?

Learning from the language of others is one way we develop our social skills, and these are complex and changing things to learn. Watching and observing what others do, and how they do it; reflecting on our emotions , how others make us feel and how our actions make others feel are key to developing social skills as a young child and at any point in our lives.

We learn about how to connect socially by watching others around us, and the environment that we are in gives us clues to this even before our active interactions begin

The roots beneath our learning and behaviours are intertwined and, if children are struggling emotionally then, whatever these emotions are, they will have a ripple onto others – they will have implications for their social connections and their social skills, their self esteem and their SELF-regualtion- and, as we know well, their SELF-regulation impacts how others see them, how others connect with them .

Rethinking our responses
There is something we need to challenge in our own practice to support these positive connections.

Occasionally, as practitioners and teachers we may have inherited inappropriate practices which were historically about keeping children in their place often suppressing opportunites for developing SELF-regulation. Yes, we do have to keep children safe, with essential boundaries, rules and routines, however it is no longer appropriate or supportive of their self-esteem or social skills to 'make them feel worse to help them behave better' I am always grateful to my esteemed colleague Kristin Wiens for sharing this strategy with me.

Thanking or Ranking?
Putting a child down in front of others or giving rewards (which help some feel good about themselves, but others feel that they are not good enough to get them) often does the opposite of supporting social skills. It makes me feel uneasy thinking about it. Rather than promoting positive behaviours, as is intended - externally imposed rewards can result in ranking children rather than thanking them for the specific skills we need to nurture, and they need to grow.

Unique Equals

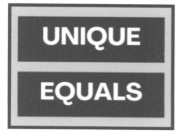

The roots of social skills are complex and ever-changing but the energy and environment we engineer around them have a powerful impact. Using the FingerTips approach gives children and their adults the resource to reflect on their skills to connect with others. One way to look at this is to consider that we are all unique equals.

Struggling socially - some ways to support

If a child is struggling socially this can stem from their SELF-regulation, have an impact on their self-esteem, learning and their behaviours - seeing things from another person's angle is a complex skill.

> # **S**upportive and Sustainable
>
> # **E**motional Implications
>
> # **E**mpathy

The acronym SEE helps us to help them to see things from another's angle. These skills are ones which could take some time to grow-in the meantime we can help them to build connections which are:

Supportive and Sustainable: Sometimes children are keen to impress others or to make new friends. I remember one little girl who had moved school who was desperate to build social connections. Every day she invited them to things which did not yet exist - a big birthday party, a trip to Legoland, a sleepover - all promises she would be unlikely to keep. These things were not supportive of a trusting relationship, neither were they realistic and sustainable.

Some children become the class clown to get themselves noticed to show they have something special. Sadly, this can attract short term social connection, but in the long term it is again, unsustainable. It often clouds an emotional and social insecurity. We need to support children in collaboration not comparison, help them feel comfortable to simply be with each other and not have to impress others, to feel confident and comfortable with themselves. This will help other children to feel comfortable and confident around them.

Emotional Implications: Helping children to see the emotional implications of their actions on others is an abstract and complex one. It is not the same as seeing the intentional impact of their actions, it is about seeing the smaller ripples, the unintentional effects on others. This is part of SELF-regulation and can take a number of years to develop. Even as adults this can be a struggle to see the implications of our actions if our own emotional roots are rocky.

Empathy: Understanding the feelings of others, being able to spot the subtleties of their body language their tone of voice come more easily to some children than to others. Some children will always find it tricky, so building in strategies that support empathy into our daily practice can make a real difference. Empathy is also about understanding how and what our own actions are communicating to others. The words may come later but their own facial expression, the way they stand and with younger children, as simple as it seems, things like pointing out that pushing is not OK can really support them in building stronger social connections and build the beginnings of self-reflection and SELF-regulation.

SELF
We have mentioned SELF-regulation a great deal, but do we have a shared understanding of what it actually is, what it actually looks like in daily life?

If you are a child SELF-regulation starts with yourself. Are you refuelled, refreshed and ready? Do they have something that makes them shine, inside and out- so that they are not always seeking the attention and approval of others?

Expected
Does the child know what is expected? Every context, every person has its own expectations and these can be difficult to read. If a child understands the importance of checking out the context, seeing from signs around them what is expected- and this is consistent this can really help overcome anxiety, build self-confidence and enable them to cope in the little journeys of daily life

Looking
How often do we dive in to a situation before we check out the context and the cues? How often do we expect children to respond to a request or question before they have had time to think. Look before you leap is a saying that has been around many years but if we can help children to pause before they 'press play' in so many contexts, this will help them be more successful and more importantly, to help them experience feeling successful.

I recommend the acronym **STAR** to adults and children alike:

Forward
Visualise and image of a road ahead- this helps us to think about what could be coming, what might surprise us and we might need to be prepared for. Learning is the longest journey and SELF-regulation is the trickiest skill for many children. If they keep on looking forward to where their actions may lead - positive , or not so positive. They can then anticipate how this will feel, how it will be feel for their friends- and begin to make their choices in a considered way, thinking of the impact on others, on their environment and on themselves.

Focusing Forward

Life is so busy and there are so many things happening at once, we need to support our children, and sometimes remind ourselves to focus on what matters most. As the adults around them, we need to know what matters most and decrease distractions around this. If we are teachers, stepping back and looking at what the child sees can help us engineer the environment in order to support the child in focusing forward

Helping children to become aware of distractions and diversions can make the world of difference to supporting their SELF-regulation

Looking Forward

For SELF-regulation children need to have experienced successes. They need to know how it feels when they have achieved something, however little, for themselves- and for that achievement to have been recognised- not rewarded but recognised- this is SO important.

> *'I was so proud of how you waited patiently while Grandma was speaking'*

> *'That pizza you made was so delicious, you took such care choosing the toppings'*

> *'You used such gentle hands when you were stroking Jason's dog - Thank you'*

If they know that persevering and being patient leads to positive thngs, and knowing how these positives feel, they are much more likely to practice this, and gradually that self-esteem and their SELF-regulation will grow. All adults agreeing what is expected, and the child knowing what is expected of them in a context, and begin to be able to spot the signs for understanding this themselves is a skill that will grow slowly. With appropriate opportunities, spotting the success and plenty of patience we can help each child on the journey from regulation, through co-regulation to SELF-regulation

©Ali McClure Education and Parenting | www.AliMcClure.co.uk | @AliMcClureEP

ROOTS OF LEARNING – COMMUNICATION AND LANGUAGE

Our children now have the tools to use to grow their own learning, but if they don't have the words that work, they may still struggle- and we may struggle to understand, to hear, what matters most to them.

With the youngest children, we will need to watch carefully, to observe how their actions and emotions are communicating their learning. With learners who are able to speak but struggle to find the right words, their confidence- the concern that they may not be able to find the right words can hold them back.

The conversation cues, help children feel confident and, even in adults, when they plan for difficult discussions, FingerTips gives them the confidence to structure their thoughts, it enables them to open up their oracy, FingerTips gives them the tools to learning, but more than that- the tools to learn (about themselves and others) through talking.

Supporting children in Ukraine

I was recently privileged to meet a woman who did incredible work supporting children and families in Ukraine. She had just a few moments before she had to present to over seven hundred people from fifty two countries around the world. She was nervous- it is hardly surprising.

She was concerned that, once she got in front of her audience she would freeze, she would forget what she had to say.

I asked if she would mind me asking her a few questions which might help her feel more confident. I used the FingerTips catalyst questions and what happened next will stay with me forever. Not only did she find the words that work, to tell me what she was particularly proud of, what helped her and the familes, what was tricky and how they tackled it etc, but her body lost its stress, her shoulders dropped, she stood up straight and spoke so confidently and coherently that, in the space of three minutes, I learned so much about her incredible work it was simply humbling.

In next to no time she knew, that if she forgot her script, she would be able to speak successfully with a passion and depth around her subject in a way that would absolutely engage her audience, and share what mattered most to her, to her children and her families.

I was so focused on the woman's experiences I did not notice the person by my side- observing the whole encounter. She stepped in , put her hand on my shoulder and said ' My friend- what you did for that woman was amazing… how did you enable her to open up like that. I explained to her that it was simply the FingerTips talking tool- and she now wants to share this simple but powerful strategy with her network- around the world!

Even if your child, or the parent at the school gate begins with one finger, one catalyst question, they can feel confident to share:

What I was particularly proud of…

What helps me…

Where can I turn when it's tricky…

What , in particular, I need to practice

What one thing can I take away today that will help me tomorrow.

Now they have the words that work and the confidence to use them, there is still more to communication- it is so complex. Communication is shared in so many other ways. Subtleties in the way they walk into the room, a flick of the eyes towards the door, a twiddling of the hair or a chewing of the sleeve. There are so many subtle signs… and the people who are able to read these best are those who have a human connection, those who know the child best. Investing time in relationships is never wasted.

Dan Hughes as part of his DDP- Dyadic, Developmental Practice uses the acronym PACE to help us develop trust with children who have experienced trauma. It is well worth looking into. Simply put, it stands for:

Playful

Acceptance

Curiousity

Empathy

This strategy helps us to see the whole child and begin to see what Dan Hughes describes as their Inner Life

As the adults around the children, one way we can communicate, often without knowing it, is through the energy we give out, and the environment we create.

ROOTS OF LEARNING – COGNITIVE CONNECTIONS

The next root is about cognitive connections. the cognitive root. It is about metacognittion, (understanding how they learn best) thinking, reasoning and remembering. It is called cognitive connections because it is about them connecting the learning across and within both hemispheres of the brain. It is also about making physical connections to their learning and making links between what they already know and what they are learning now. Making links makes learning last, makes learning matter.

Understanding how they learn, and having young children think things through before they act may seem like advanced skills - but from the earliest age, if we can empower them to reflect on their learning, what makes it successful and what helps them to overcome problems, they will build their own bank of strategies. They will develop the skills and importantly the questions to ask of themselves in order to learn how they learn, to consolidate that metacognition, those cognitive connections, for now and for life.

Let's reflect on how the **FingerTips** tool supports metacognition:

'What were you particularly proud of?'
Simply taking the time to reflect is the first step. Knowing the importance of talking through the process and the progress not simply celebrating a product.

'What were you particularly proud of?' helps them think of the details, specifically what they have achieved, what went well and how they went about it.

'What helped you?' or 'Who helped you?'
(Positive partners, processes or props)
This helps them to notice that certain tools, certain strategies and certain people are powerful in supporting their success. If they can dive deeper and work out how these things helped and why they had such an impact, this really supports their metacognition and helps them to understand their own learning, grow their own learning and own their own learning. Having agency with metacognition is such a powerful combination. With younger children, if this tool helps us to better understand what best supports their learning, we are better empowered to help them grow.

What was tricky... and how did I tackle it?
'What was tricky?' Knowing from an early age that learning is the longest journey and always includes stumbling and struggling. Knowing that even the most successful people suffer setbacks is simply empowering. Being able to say *'Constructing my corners was tricky, but this is how I tackled it'* equips them and those who are listening, with skills for the future with ways to understand their own learning- metacognition In almost every case, leaving them feeling positive about their problem-solving skills is important and a good place to stop.

But this is where the adults need to use their wisdom; there are some situations where the steps the child took did not solve the problem and we must never leave them feeling like they are failures - in these cases then the next question is *'What else could you try to tackle this?'* or *'Who would you turn to tackle this together?'*

Who would you turn to to tackle this together?
Learning is always the longest journey with bumps along the way; we must ensure that the children know that, as much as they build the skills to bounce back, they should never have to walk this journey of learning alone. As adults it is our responsibility to join them on their journey, knowing when to step in, when to step back and when to step up. Feeling supported but not stifled, will give the children the confidence to own their own learning but be brave enough to take those reasonable and reasoned risks which allow them to strive, stumble and then succeed.

Know when to step in,
When to step back
When to step up

All through this discovery dialogue, with a partner, an adult or simply with themselves, children are learning how they learn and how they can use this information to shape their behaviours and their future learning. Each child is learning about themselves, but they are also giving the adults an insight into how they learn best. Even better, the implications for others of all ages listening are that they will be learning the tools, skills and practices that may well empower them in their own learning.

FingerTips is a reflective learners' talking tool, but the listeners are learning too.
It empowers everyone to know their own learning - grow their own learning.
It gives everyone the agency and oracy to show their own learning - to share their own learning.

Repetition of the Right Thing...
What is the right thing for this learner, at this time, in this context?

A young child might need help in pinpointing what they need to practice, the part which requires repetition. An adult might help them break their learning down into smaller steps or if they are very young, decide on the right things to repeat for them. This skill is perfectly possible for children and develops as we talk, learn and grow; but however old we get, talking to a partner about the specific steps to practice helps us to shine a light on the specifics of learning which will be most helpful, which will benefit us most by repeating.

LInked Learning- Making learning last

Making links between already embedded learning and what we have just learned is what makes learning last. It helps children categorise and connect their learning making it easier to retrieve. Linking little fingers helps children to reflect on specifically what they have learned today and, again when they start their learning next time. That physical gesture can trigger the memory of their previous learning and bring it back afresh ready for them to begin their learning eager and empowered. The habit of linking little fingers at the start of their learning helps build this reflective practice.

Cognitive load - 'How wide is your windscreen?'

Choosing just one thing to remember also helps those who may struggle with their cognitive load. This is a grand term so to make it easier to envisage, I view cognitive load through the question *'How wide is your windscreen?'*. Depending on what is happening in our own little world, then the windscreen though which we view our learning may be narrower or wider. If we are in a good place, then our windscreen is wider there is more space for learning to be embedded. If we are not so well rooted at the moment, then the windscreen through which we view our learning will be narrower.

There are various theories as to how many pieces of learning we can take on board at once, whichever of these you subscribe to, the bottom line is always, how wide is the windscreen for this particular child at this particular time? Imagine the learning as post-it notes. If your windscreen is narrow, there is space for only very few of these to stick allowing you still to be able to see out. If you are in a positive place, with your physical, emotional and social connections firmly rooted then your windscreen is likely to be wide enough to allow several post-its to stick. Whether your windscreen is wide or if you are struggling to see out, using our linked little fingers to recall just one important aspect of linked learning enables every child to remember one thing that helps them to learn, and to begin their learning in a positive place next time.

Intertwined and interconnected

All the roots are intertwined and have implications on our learning. We don't simply build cognitive connections with the conventional curriculum subjects, we also build cognitive connections about our strategy in social situations, about how we look after our own emotional wellbeing, how we manage our own emotional regulation and even recognising our deep-seated needs for the physical aspects of learning. Metacognition helps us to reflect and connect with our learning, our behaviours and our learning behaviours...

The roots of learning are intertwined.

- and **FingerTips** empowers us to equip our children, step by step, with the language and skills to do just this, with **the language of learning for life!**

ROOTS OF LEARNING - CONTEXT AND CHANGE

The roots of learning, or what is beneath their behaviours lie beneath the surface. In our plant and root image, these are in the soil. We have reflected on the roots but how often do we consider the context, and change- the things that are in the soil; things which happen to the children over which they have little or no control

We have spoken already about the context of the child and about how as the adults around them we build the emotional environment for our children. The context to think about here is about how children interact with the context they are in and especially the changing contexts: transitions and new environments, new places and new people. Something as simple as changing activities or timings can make them anxious or unsetlled, - a change in the people in their lives can certainly have an impact

Helping children to understand how they cope with change can help them prepare for things they might consider a challenge - a change of activity, a change of plan, a change of house, school, town, country... the list goes on.

When change feels challenging - supportive, sustainable strategies

How we interact with change in our lives can help us predict and plan - enabling us to know we have the tools to support us through tricky transitions. The following may seem like a list of strategies which can simply support children effectively in their schools or settings, but like the majority of effective strategies, they actually work throughout life. They are seemingly simple actions and words but are actually supportive and sustainable strategies which again empower us and the children with the language of learning for life...

ROOTS OF LEARNING – ENERGY AND ENVIRONMENT

Energy and Environment
These are the things that we add to the soil, that have an unseen impact on the way the children and adults around us feel- and ultimately, the way they behave. I learned this several years ago and it stops me short every time I question why a child is behaving as they are.

Reading the room
In every new context they encounter, children and adults alike have to learn to 'read the room' They need to observe, watch, wait and listen to see what is expected; what is accepted and what is acceptable.

We need to be aware of our influence on the child's environment, on the energy that we are emitting, the energy in the room . Our influence and the implications of our actions, have such a powerful impact on the child, their learning, behaviour and learning behaviours - as well as their self-esteem and well-being.

Grown-ups can often walk away from their workplace if they are unhappy or anxious. Children don't have this luxury. We curate the conditions for their learning, we curate the curriculum, the continuous provision, the challenges and the communication. This is a powerful and privileged position.

Deliberate decisions
As responsible adults we need to challenge our choices and those of others around us. We need to check that our practices are purposefully chosen, not untimely, inappropriate or simply inherited. We need to be certain that the decisions we make are deliberately taken, for that context, for that child... and what better tool to use to reflect on our own practice than...
FingerTips!

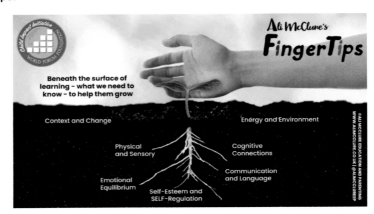

SEEMINGLY SIMPLE STRATEGIES- WITH A DEPTH THAT MAKES THE DIFFERENCE

STRATEGY	YOUNG CHILD	ADOLESCENT	ADULT	HOW IT MAKES THEM FEEL	WHY IT WORKS
Transitions, Instructions and Implications - When it is difficult to move from one activity to another, or to follow instructions... When they do not understand the implications of their action – or inaction.					
When... then.... (avoid 'If you don't do this you won't be able to do that) (Keep to connected positive consequences- avoid extrinsic and imposed rewards or punishments)	When you have put your shoes on,then we can go to the park. When the sand timer is empty, then you need to put on your coat	When you have passed your exam, then you can get into the college you have chosen	When you have paid the bill, then you can have your new car	It helps them to understand the reason why a change is necessary. It helps them to feel the anticipation of the positive outcome	It plants positive pictures in their minds. It helps them to focus on an outcome which is of intrinsic importance to them. Purpose not punishment- it empowers children to know the reasons why they are doing things rather than relying on extrinsic rewards or punishment

STRATEGY	YOUNG CHILD	ADOLESCENT	ADULT	HOW IT MAKES THEM FEEL	WHY IT WORKS
Keeping some control - When it causes anxiety to change from one activity to another... When they want to feel they have some control... When they want to be able to plan how to spend their time and think ahead...					
Now... Next...	Now we are having a snack, next it is story time Visual symbols displayed in chronological order removed by the child when completed	Station information displayed on a train journey or children making their own timeline 'to do' list	Calendar or timetable for the workday or week TV schedule	Confident that they know what is coming next- what is expected and what they can expect	Anxiety is overcome, or at least planned for so that they can feel prepared. It helps them prepare for things coming to a close and feel some control as this time approaches

Section B – Diving Deeper

STRATEGY	YOUNG CHILD	ADOLESCENT	ADULT	HOW IT MAKES THEM FEEL	WHY IT WORKS
Struggling to make a start - When they are feeling anxious or finding it difficult to do something new to them... (perhaps they suffer with anxiety, lack confidence or have additional needs)					
Breaking it down backwards	In learning to put their own coat on: Pull up the zip the final tug to the top. Next pull up the zip from the bottom. Next put the two parts of the zip together	In beginning to travel a train journey to college alone: Accompanied at a distance - they keep their ticket safe and exit the barrier alone. Next, they watch out for and get off at the correct stop. Next, they read the rail information and get on the correct train.	In beginning to lock up the shop at the end of the day. They turn the key in the lock. Next, they set the alarm and .... Next, they put the takings in the safe, set the alarm...	They feel a sense of achievement every time they try, however long this takes. They feel confident and begin to be able to apply this skill to other tasks- metacognition!	They experience the final steps first, meaning that as they develop the skills there will never be a final hurdle to overcome. This builds in success

STRATEGY	YOUNG CHILD	ADOLESCENT	ADULT	HOW IT MAKES THEM FEEL	WHY IT WORKS
Seeking some structure - When they feel uncertain as things change unpredictably... When they struggle to form helpful habits... When they have little structure in their lives and struggle with this....					
Routine. Regular things happening at regular times in a day or week or month. These should not be restrictive nor overly rigorous but do need to be predictable patterns and seen as permanent (until the children or the context outgrow them)	Bedtimes, story times, teeth cleaning, mealtimes. Special one to one time- with parent, carer, key person or grandparent	Bedtimes, mealtimes, special one to one time, homework time, exercise time, screens off time	Exercise time, relaxation time, connection time, screens off time	Predictable patterns help children feel safe. They help them to overcome anxiety of what is coming next. Routines help them to feel empowered and they have more agency over their own time and actions	We all need rhythm in our lives and routines that are well matched offer a supportive structure. They help children build other things around the routines they can rely on building independence and self-regulation

Section B – Diving Deeper

STRATEGY	YOUNG CHILD	ADOLESCENT	ADULT	HOW IT MAKES THEM FEEL	WHY IT WORKS
When things go wrong, or patterns change unexpectedly causing stress or anxiety…					
Whoops card or whoops moment or whoops gesture. Adults getting into the habit of using a consistent, card, gesture or phrase when unpredicted things happen or things go wrong- and modelling calm positive, problem-solving behaviour	When a drink is spilled	When the bus doesn't come	When the internet goes down. Diversion signs, hazard triangles and blue lights are all real-world examples of the whoops card	Reassured, that this is different- but it will be OK. Comforted that the adult knows that something has changed, and they are with us through this wobble	It lets a child know that things do change unexpectedly, or not go as we might hope and that is OK. We can cope, we can become more resilient to these whoops times and know how to navigate inconveniences

STRATEGY	YOUNG CHILD	ADOLESCENT	ADULT	HOW IT MAKES THEM FEEL	WHY IT WORKS
Step by Step - When learning the rules and routines in a new situation or context…					
Step by step- If we are helping a child change routine or become familiar with a new context it is helpful to introduce them to small aspects of this first – then build when they are confident and sufficiently accomplished with that step	One area of the reception playground is set up to begin, others are only added when the children are ready to progress	In learning to drive, the learner is taken to a safe car park to simply learn to start and stop	In a new job an apprentice is taught about one area first and progresses when they show confidence and competence in this.	This makes them feel confident in each step before they progress onto the next. It helps them to feel safe, and develop self-esteem, as they have experienced success	This strategy builds in success. Progression only occurs when the child is ready for it- judged by a wise adult, teacher or mentor. It also ensures that skills are learned effectively and embedded before new expectations are added

STRATEGY	YOUNG CHILD	ADOLESCENT	ADULT	HOW IT MAKES THEM FEEL	WHY IT WORKS
New Beginnings - When they are anxious about beginning a new setting, school or job…					
Advance information: transition book, guidebook or welcome video tour	Picture book showing their peg, seat, classroom, teacher, playground, toilet, lunch space, school pet etc.	They can see the options available at their new sixth form college, the facilities, the options, the clubs, the rules and expectations	Video tour shows the personality of their new workplace. A handbook shares dos and don'ts so they know enough to start without having to ask too many questions. They don't feel like 'The new boy'	They feel safer that they know where the toilets are, where to eat, where they will sit. They learn subtle clues from the places and people in the information letting them know they will be safe and soon will be happy there. They learn essential rules to keep them safe, so they feel less likely to make mistakes	They are able to picture themselves in this situation. They see things which are familiar to them-making cognitive and emotional connections. They see things they know they like and can ask questions about things that might be new to them

STRATEGY	YOUNG CHILD	ADOLESCENT	ADULT	HOW IT MAKES THEM FEEL	WHY IT WORKS
Scared to seek support - When they are nervous in a new situation, or worried to ask questions about what they need…					
Buddy - an established, empathetic and patient person or older child who is happy to show them how their new world works and to be happy to answer any questions	Simply another child to play with, sit with, eat with. To show them the ropes and around their new environment	An established student or team member who can show the new person ways to fit in easily, how to behave in certain contexts and good places to go- for support or socialising	A co-worker who will not judge when there are questions to be asked or mistakes are made. Not a line manager or someone feeding back to authority. Simply a supporter	It helps them not to feel worried if they do not know what to do or how to behave. It helps them to feel more confident to join in and talk to others	This person literally 'joins them on their journey'. They become their 'special someone' at least until they are settled and feel comfortable and confident. They help them understand their new context and make positive connections

Section B – Diving Deeper

STRATEGY	YOUNG CHILD	ADOLESCENT	ADULT	HOW IT MAKES THEM FEEL	WHY IT WORKS
Reassuring rules - with reasons - When they are anxious that they might not get it right, or if they find it hard to remember and relate to the rules…					
The right amount of rules (and the reasoning behind them) - strategies to keep everyone safe based on respect for all and the shared values of the specific setting	In a bigger school - walk on the left in the corridors	When starting University - always have an emergency number in your phone	In a new country - have a sticker on the windscreen remining you to drive on the right	The right rules and understanding the reasoning behind them helps them feel more confident to try new things and most importantly, to feel safe.	A few simple, sensible rules are memorable, especially when you know the reasoning behind the rules and how that helps everyone keep safe

STRATEGY	YOUNG CHILD	ADOLESCENT	ADULT	HOW IT MAKES THEM FEEL	WHY IT WORKS
Knowing what is 'expected' - When they are anxious that they might not get it right, or if they as struggling to read the signs and expectations of the context rules…					
Knowing what is 'expected' rather than simply different adults' expectations, helps everyone to follow the appropriate example of others, follow positive patterns and build in success for their social strategies- growing in confidence in all kinds of different contexts and settings	At mealtime, - knowing that it is expected that they finish their main course before they are allowed dessert	When they are teenagers, knowing what is expected by the adults around them for use of their phone or screentime	In a new job, knowing what dress code is expected for certain events	Being able to read the context, looking, listening and learning what is 'expected' helps them feel more confident to try new things and most importantly, to feel safe. It also helps the adults around them feel confident that they are consistent	The word 'expected' rather than 'expectations' builds consistency and encourages conversations around what are shared values, what is accepted, appropriate and acceptable- to all concered.

Respectful reminders and quiet correction - When they have made a mistake in a new setting....

STRATEGY	YOUNG CHILD	ADOLESCENT	ADULT	HOW IT MAKE THEM FEEL	WHY IT WORKS
Respectful reminders, Quiet correction, Unconditional positive regard	We walk on the left to keep us safe	It is important to have an emergency number and to let us know how we can contact you- to keep you safe	In a place where it might be easy to forget, a simple sign to anticipate errors and remind 'Keep Right'	It makes them feel respected, trusted, worth guiding to get it right. We never need to humiliate or intimidate. We never need to make them feel worse to get them to behave better- this makes them feel terrible about themselves and undermines their roots of learning and the connections with the adults.	Many of us think in pictures. Respectfully reminding them of the positive rules embeds that picture in their mind. We are all fallible and, for whatever reason make mistakes. Knowing that they are not a bad person because they have made a mistake, especially when they are new to a context helps them to build resilience and skills towards self-regulation

SECTION C

TAKING OUR FINGERTIPS EVEN FURTHER

TAKING YOUR LEARNING FURTHER

Congratulations! You are now ready to take your learning, and the learning of those you are privileged to grow, even further. Behaviour, learning and language are inextricably linked and the **FingerTips** approach to reflective learning grew out of something bigger, the Five Fundamentals for Building Brilliant Behaviour. We use the word behaviour on an everyday basis, but what does it actually mean?

My suggestion is that:

Behaviour is simply how they show -
What it is they need to grow!

In other words, the behaviour is underpinned by the learning, and we do not learn in isolation.

Important interactions
In life there are always groups of people we need to interact with and most of us work or play amongst others.

We have focused much on the individual up to now. This next level of learning, for the child and for their important adults helps us look at how we interact with others, how we **'KNOW IT, GROW IT AND SHOW IT'** both for ourselves and for our colleagues and companions.

So, let's take our learning further and discover how our **FingerTips** talking tool can help us extend the learning and language of those we work with, not just for now but for life

THUMBS UP

This is the **CONVERSATION CUE** for
'What are you particularly proud of?'

The child might respond:
'I am particularly proud of how I...'

or

'I feel pride inside that I tried... '

Being a team player
We are now practised in this, but there is more. The next step in this discovery dialogue takes us back to our gesture. The thumbs up - but this time lets focus on the four fingers curled around. While the thumb represents the individual, these four fingers represent the team.

'What are the team particularly proud of? 'What do they feel pride inside that they tried?'

'They worked together and organised the bake sale'

These **CONVERSATION CUES** and **CATALYST QUESTIONS** help the child with their empathy, co-operative and team building skills, enabling them to think of the bigger picture, of the team rather than simply the individual.

What part did I play?
The final step again refers back to the hand position. The thumbs up. This time focus back on the thumb and ask the child to tuck it inside the four fingers. This represents the child's part in the team - an even more advanced concept.

'What part did you play in the team? | 'What aspect of that are you particularly proud of?' | 'What do you feel pride inside that you tried?'

'I was the artist- it was my job to design the poster'

Truly working as a trusted team member needs a certain level of maturity and is based on strong and sound relationships, something we nurture for our children as they grow. As we encourage our children to reflect using the three levels suggested by the thumb- self, the team and my part in the team, we might consider if this approach to reflecting on teamwork and the relationships within it might be useful when coaching some of our colleagues, or when reflecting for ourselves.

THE POINTING INDEX FINGER

In pointing our finger - in a positive way, we remember that the **CATALYST QUESTION** for this **CONVERSATION CUE** is

'Who helped you?' or *'What helped you?'*

This is probably one of the earliest conversation cues that children can grasp.'

Three fingers pointing back at us!
The index finger is pointing to the thing or the person that helped. Looking back at the hand - when there is one finger pointing away from us, there are three fingers tucked in which are pointing back at ourselves. What did we do with that advice, with that equipment?

So, when a child is ready to think more deeply, to move on to the next level we could consider asking *'So Jenna showed you how to use the protractor - how did you go on to use it?'*

The focus here is not the finger pointing at the person or thing that helped them, but the three fingers tucked into the palm and pointing back at themselves.

'Sophie helped you by sharing her crayons with you. How did this help you?...
What did you do next?'

Paying it forward...
We want to promote a culture of reflecting and learning, not just for ourselves but looking at how we can help others. The final stage with the index finger is *'So, know you have learned this, what would you do to help someone else who might be finding the same thing tricky?'*

In every trade, profession or hobby, paying it forward and supporting others when they may be struggling or in need of new strategies is how one generation supports the next.

An unusual hobby I know, but my son happens to have grown up in the world of magic. When he was fourteen and was building his first stage show, one of the best-known magicians gave him considerable time, support and guidance to help him grow his show. As a grateful parent I so appreciated this wisdom and support, I asked this magician how we could recompense him for his time. He thanked us for our kindness but replied that it would be down to Callum to thank him - passing on the legacy by giving generously to the next generation of magicians when he was established and experienced. I feel particularly proud that he is now doing just that.

I have seen this so many times in many professions and in hobbies but in everyday experiences too, cooking, DIY, maths - in fact, this **FingerTips** approach applies to almost anything that can be learned in life.

When we become reflective learners, it equips and empowers us to later become responsive teachers. The two are inextricably intertwined.

THE BUMPY MIDDLE FINGER

The longest journey
Remember as you reach out your middle finger it represents the longest journey with the knuckles representing the bumps along the way.

Our initial **CONVERSATION CUE** prompted the reflection

'What was tricky and how did you tackle it?'

or

'How do you bounce back when the road gets bumpy?'

These reflections are fine, but they are deliberately simplistic. The next level helps children to see greater depth, relate back to the roots of their challenges and how they overcame them. The problem might not simply be a practical one but about how they feel, rather than just what they are learning.

Reflect on their emotional equilibrium
In response to your question 'What did you find tricky today?' their reflective response might be 'I found it tricky to concentrate today'. If you feel they are ready to dive deeper and reflect on their emotional equilibrium in a safe place to do so you could ask:

'How did this make you feel?'

The child, if they have heard others use the language of learning for emotions, might respond

'It made me feel frustrated - I was not able to get on with my story'.

The conversation might continue –

'How did you overcome this problem?'

'I put on my ear defenders and was able to focus'.

The great thing about this strategy is that when children share that they have challenges, others pay attention, they think that *'They are just like me - I might be able to learn from them'* and they do. With this **CONVERSATION CUE** in particular the children are becoming reflective learners, but they also impact on the other children by extending their emotional language, their reflective response, enabling others to grow these skills too.

From self to others
If you hold your horizontal middle pointing away from you its tip is the furthest point from your body. This finger represents the longest journey, and the journey from self to others, a simple summary of what SELF-regulation is about, shifting our focus from ourselves to be able to think of our impact on ourselves and on others, what was tricky for our team and how we can work together to overcome this.

Supportive space
If relationships are raised in these reflections, these are sensitive, so it's best to make an opportunity to reflect on this personally with the child, in a safe and supportive space.

SELF-regulation
In the Five Fundamentals for Brilliant Behaviour, where the **FingerTips** approach originated, the middle finger is about being ready and responsive, resilient, resourceful and ready for action.

These characteristics are all supportive of strong relationships but are also the skills of SELF-regulation. This complex concept is one that we may well think we have mastered, until times are tough, things go wrong, or we are unwell or unhappy. Then we can all struggle with our SELF-regulation at any age and... will need support.

To step in or take a step back?

In leading these conversations, we need to reflect - at this particular time do they need our support and we need to step in, or are they ready to take the next steps for themselves? It is our insight and understanding of the individual and their current context that helps us to make this decision- and that is the craft of the very best coaches and teachers.

Taking their learning further

The final level of depth is that, in tracing your finger along the back of your middle finger you have only reached the knuckle. There is always further to go. Frustrating sometimes, but always true - the journey of learning is never complete!

The catalyst question here would be:

'What do you think might still be tricky?'

'How do you feel about that?'

'How do you think you might solve that problem?'

and importantly

'Who can you turn to join you on your journey, to support you when you stumble?'

Everyone needs a hand to hold

The important lesson here is we never embark on a tricky journey without knowing who we have to support us.

Everyone needs a 'hand to hold', someone who knows
when to step up,
when to step back and
when to step up to support.

With this in place we will feel able to take those first steps to tackle what's tricky - steps that will lead us closer to success- whatever that looks like for us.

THE FOURTH FINGER - REPETITION OF THE RIGHT THING

The power of practice
The ring on this finger represents something that is repeated. What is it that we need to repeat at this particular time?

Linking back to the Five Fundamentals this is about the right relationships and well as the right routines

It is about how practice makes things permanent (not perfect!) and frees up space in our working memories to be able to make more meaningful connections, with people and with learning.

The initial **CATALYST QUESTION** asks

'What have you practised that has helped you today?'

Strategies for practice
Successful practice is a skill that needs to be learned. Questioning further if we know the learner is ready, we can ask

'What helped you to practice?'

'How did you remember to practice?'

'What did you do when you didn't feel like practising?'

Seen to be successful
When a child who is seen to be successful talks about what, when, how and why they practice, this makes those children whose skills have been a little slower to grow prick up their ears. So often we only see the successes of children who are not visibly seen to struggle. When we learn that actually, those who are successful do practice, and know they need to practice, that gives us mere mortals faith that, we too can improve our skills, make progress through our practice and soon begin to achieve some hard-earned success.

Help to progress
When something is working well it becomes a habit, a regular routine. These routines are rather like cogs and, after all cogs are simply wheels that fit together well. So, we can encourage children to reflect on what they have repeated and maybe not even noticed that has helped them progress and made their performance become more permanent, more reliable.

In the Five Fundamentals for Brilliant Behaviour the fourth finger is about reliability - rules routines and relationships we can rely on.

Practice partners?
They can also consider who helps them to practice, - does practising with a friend make a difference, sticking to a specific time, or going to a different place?

Regular repetition
Regular repetition can also play a part in this, and just like cogs, the best habits, practice and routines are things which repeat regularly, they have a pattern and soon become helpful habits.

HEALTH WARNING - this is not about homework for homework's sake. The practice should be carefully chosen and never become a chore. It is specifically about pinpointing the right thing for that child to repeat, in a way that works for them and that they will be able to see the purpose of the practice by the progress they are experiencing for themselves when they next share with their FingerTips.

Focus for the future
In the final stage for this ring finger our focus shifts to the future - 'Having heard what others have practised, have a think how you could use practice to take your learning further- what you might want to practise in the future'

This is something that the children can reflect on in their own heads – take a pause- no need to respond. Let them know they can turn to you if they need some suggestions or support with this, that you are always happy to join them on their journey.

Curating the questions
This particular **CONVERSATION CUE** shows just how deep these discovery dialogues can go, and it makes an important point - that the questions need curating. They need to be matched to the moment and the group or individual you are working with. As the important adult posing the catalyst questions, we need to choose the one or two that are right for that time, that place, that child, that learner. Each one works alone or in combination with others. This is part of why this approach is so powerful and promotes personalised learning that lasts.

Avoid logging every comment
What you as the adult, the teacher, the mentor or the coach do with the information this reflective learning tool gives you is down to your professional judgement. I would encourage you to avoid having pen and paper to hand and certainly not logging every comment into a computer. It is not a data-gathering exercise - it is important that you make time, model effective listening, open and positive body language for every child at every stage of their journey of learning. There will, however, be key things that you learn about the children, every time these conversation cues are used.

Reflect and connect
I would encourage you to reflect about how you will use this information to inform your interactions and interventions, how you will use this information to curate your curriculum, your questioning and your continuous provision - the learning resources for that child. I would encourage you to reflect on how you can use this information to support the child in their SELF-regulation, learning and behaviours. I would also encourage you to use what you have learned to connect with others who share the care for that child.

Reflecting and connecting is what our last conversation cue links together so simply but so effectively. Whichever questions you have asked, however deep you have dived, whether working with an individual, a group, a child and adult or simply reflecting for yourself, a good way to end is with the linked little fingers.

LINKED LITTLE FINGERS - LINKED LEARNING

Making the connection to retrieve the learning
Some children have named this gesture the 'Pinkie Promise'
It is the one thing they will remember by linking
their little fingers together.

It is simple but it helps the learning to stick, after all, our
memory is about making connections to retrieve the
learning from the far corners and filing systems of our brains.

We make that connection tangible by linking our little fingers
together.

Adding a picture or a place
Diving deeper, encourage the child to attach this memory to a picture or a place. Ask the child to spot what they can see when they are linking their fingers, ask them to remember who they were with, or focus on how they feel. All these things can link our memory to our senses and emotions, it makes them easier to retrieve.

Do a little dance
I only recently discovered that when my youngest son is helping himself to remember something he does a little dance - he then remembers where he was when he did the dance. If we connect our fingers and move them around this has a similar effect - What could we see? What did we feel?

The power of this **CONVERSATION CUE** is the linking - it helps the learner and the teacher. It means that learning goes on - into the next time - when, at the start of the session the children link their little fingers and their memory takes them right back, to the place, the feelings and the strategy that they have selected for themselves that empowers them to make a start.

So, the linked learning little fingers connect the cycle - it closes today and starts tomorrow enabling every child to be prepared, use their learning time well and make the progress that is right for them.

Helping the teacher
I mentioned that the linking of fingers also helps the teacher - when a child is reflecting on their previous learning, they use the gestures to help them remember - the teacher can see at a glance what the children across their class are discussing; the gestures show their thinking! Even the littlest learners begin to use the gestures and soon start to share them with parents.

FINGERTIPS INTO THE FUTURE

Embedded, empowering and essential
The FingerTips reflective learners' talking tool becomes contagious- in the most positive of ways. Learners and teachers of all ages and at all stages begin to use it and share it as part of their day-to-day practice. Before you know it, the FingerTips approach becomes embedded and an essential part of 'Everybody's Everyday'.

FingerTips for future planning
The families I work with have taken FingerTips one step further, they have begun to use it for future planning:

- *'Thinking of the new term, what do you hope you will be particularly proud of?'*

- *'What do you think will help you? What has helped you before?'*

- *'What might be tricky? How might you tackle it?'*

- *'What do you think you have practised that might help you? What routines have you got in place that might be useful'*

- *'What one thing are you going to remember as you start your new term?'*

Flexibility and focus
I hesitate when calling FingerTips, a formula as much of its strength lies in its flexibility. It is more of an approach that becomes stronger the more it is embedded into your 'everyday.' You can choose how many of the conversation cues and catalyst questions to use.

You can leave your catalyst questions open, allowing learners to show us what matters most, even if it is not what you had anticipated!

Or you can narrow the focus and start with a contextual question:

- *'Today, thinking of how you have worked as a team- what are you particularly proud of?'*

- *'Today, thinking of how you have used practical props, what has helped you?'*

- *'Today, thinking of your letter formation, what have you found tricky - how did you tackle this?'*

- *'Today, thinking of your skills in fielding, what have you practised and what might you practise for next time?'*
- *'Today, thinking of what helps you feel confident in making a start, what one thing will you put in place next time'*

Having a particular focus is especially helpful if you are connecting and reflecting on the journey of a person or child who does not currently have the language to reflect for themselves; simply think of a focus from their roots of learning and imagine the words they would use if they were able.

Reflecting on a collaborative event
Either as adults or even with our children we might reflect on an event. Rather than focusing on the individual's efforts, this is a time to tweak the first catalyst question. 'What went well?' or 'What is going well' are the most effective questions in this context. This is only for when there is no teacher involved-when there is no hidden agenda of second guessing what the leader may want to hear.

Take it in your direction

Growing this strategy has been a process, it has evolved and developed and with any learning it is a journey. If you choose to join me on this journey you will take it in the direction that works for you, for your children, your school, your setting or your workplace. You may choose to use it with your own family, your team members or simply as a tool to empower you to better understand your own journey, have the tools to use and the words to work to feel confident in your oracy and feel empowered by your agency.

Problems and pitfalls

As with any journey there are problems and pitfalls - I only have three for you to be alert to:

- Finger number three- the longest journey- We must always prepare the child for this catalyst question by using a positive one first (the thumb or index finger work well). But most importantly, the middle finger must always have a resolution - never simply stop with what's tricky but go on to talk though how to tackle it. . Consider the child's feelings and leave the learner feeling positive and that the way forward is perfectly possible.

- We need to be sensitive to the child who is not sharing or over-sharing, their challenges may be more personal, and you will need to offer a supportive space, person and time to talk this through with them and steering them towards the support they need.

- It is essential to avoid the strategy becoming stale, so how you choose to use it depends on you, and you will soon discover - on your children. It is a resilient strategy, it is perfectly possible to neglect it, leave it for a while then come back to it. It is perfectly possible to use just one finger, one conversation cue.

The language of learning ... for life!

Do start off by modelling FingerTips in your own reflections, embed it into your everyday practice - then simply embrace it as part of your connecting and reflecting culture. Once it has been embedded it can be used how and when it is needed. The FingerTips reflective learning tool simply becomes the language of learning... for life!

I would love to know how the approach works for you - positives, problems or pitfalls or welcome you to join me on some FingerTips training.

You can find out more via the website **www.alimcclure.co.uk** or contact us on **office@alimcclure.co.uk** to take your learning even further with **FingerTips**.

About the Author

Children, the way they learn and why they behave as they do are Ali McClure's life's work and passion. Ali is particularly proud of the research, insight and impact that have gone into growing her unforgettable FingerTips strategy. She has been writing, teaching and speaking for more than two decades to countless educators and families in the UK and across the globe. Her lively delivery and inspirational work on 'Supporting Self-Regulation and SEND', 'Learning through Play, Bringing Play to their Learning' and 'Building Brilliant Behaviours' are highly acclaimed, with the FingerTIps approach recently recognised by the Centre for International Research at Eton College England and the World Forum Child Impact Initiative. Previously known for her timeless book 'Making it Better for Boys', Ali is an award-winning consultant, creator and changemaker. Being a SENCo and teaching and tutoring young children, helping them and the adults around them find supportive, sustainable solutions is important to her, and keeps her practice current. Ali specialises in helping every child and the adults around them to believe in themselves and to achieve... whatever their challenges may be. Her strategies are simply, supportive and sustainable- growing with the child and working for learners of all ages.

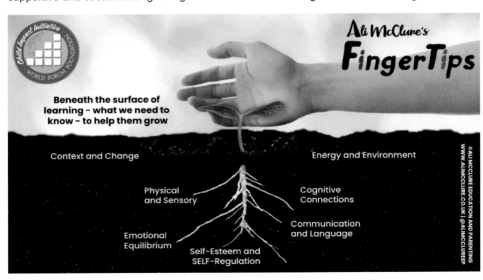